Welcome to the Halloween Joke Book!

Thank you for choosing our book to add some Halloween fun to your child's day! We hope your little one enjoys the spooky and funny jokes inside.

Get ready to embark on a fun-filled journey into the realm of Halloween jokes! This book is packed with silly, spooky, and downright hilarious jokes that will tickle your funny bone and brighten your Halloween celebrations. Whether you're at a Halloween party, trick-or-treating with friends, or just looking to share a laugh, these jokes are perfect for every child.

So grab your favorite pumpkin spice treat, find a cozy spot, and let the giggles begin! Happy Haunting!

60 FREE Halloween Jokes Inside!

To Everyone Enjoying the Halloween Spirit This Year!

Hey Parents! Ready to make this Halloween extra special? We've got a spooktacular treat just for you and your little one!

60 FREE Halloween Jokes!

Your child will love these exclusive Jokes all inspired by our book. Are you ready to unleash your inner comedian? Flip through these pages to discover 60 free Halloween jokes that are sure to make you and your friends roar with laughter! It's the perfect way to keep the Halloween spirit alive and boost creativity!

Here's a sneak peek:

- What do you call a monster who poisons corn flakes?
  A cereal killer!

- Why didn't the skeleton go to the party?
  Because he had no body to go with!

Getting them is easy:

Just scan the QR code above to instantly download your free pages. It's fast, simple, and sure to bring smiles all around!

Share Your Experience!

If You Laugh, You Lose!

Think you can handle all the jokes in this book? Prove it! If you laugh, you lose! But don't worry—losing is a blast!

Here's how to join the fun in just 30 seconds:

1. **Open your camera app.**
2. **Point it at the QR code on the right.**
3. **Boom!** The review page opens instantly!

Let us know which jokes made you laugh the hardest! Share your thoughts, and you might just inspire other little monsters to join the fun!

© 2024 by Anthony J. Trice. All Rights Reserved.

This book is protected by copyright law. No part of this publication may be reproduced, distributed, or transmitted in any form or by any means, including photocopying, recording, or other electronic or mechanical methods, without the prior written permission of the publisher, except in the case of brief quotations embodied in critical reviews and certain other non-commercial uses permitted by copyright law.

HOW DO VAMPIRES GET AROUND ON HALLOWEEN?

On blood vessels.

WHY DID THE HEADLESS HORSEMAN GET A JOB?

He was trying to get ahead in life.

HOW CAN YOU TELL WHEN A VAMPIRE HAS BEEN IN A BAKERY?

All the jelly has been sucked out of the jelly doughnuts.

WHAT DO GHOSTS WEAR WHEN THEIR EYESIGHT GETS BLURRED?

Spooktacles.

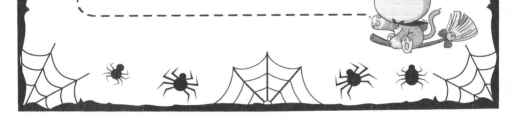

WHAT CAN YOU CATCH FROM A VAMPIRE IN WINTER?

Frostbite.

WHAT WOULD BE THE NATIONAL HOLIDAY FOR A NATION OF VAMPIRES?

Fangs-giving!

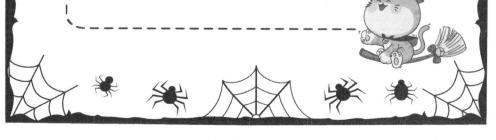

WHY DIDN'T THE SKELETON GO TO PROM?

He had no body to go with.

WHO DID THE SCARY GHOST INVITE TO HIS PARTY?

Any old friend he could dig up!

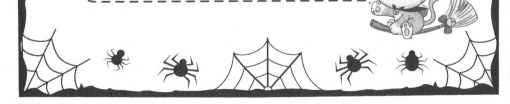

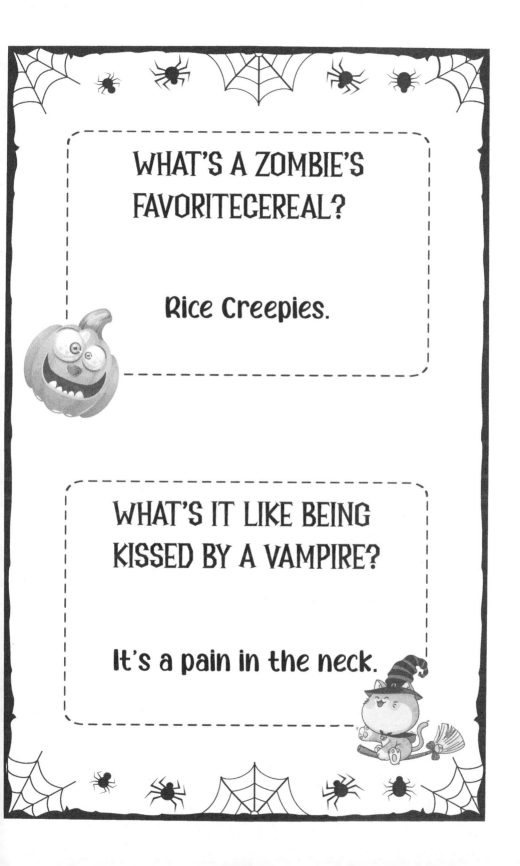

WHAT'S A ZOMBIE'S
FAVORITECEREAL?

Rice Creepies.

WHAT'S IT LIKE BEING
KISSED BY A VAMPIRE?

It's a pain in the neck.

WHERE DO GHOSTS GO ON HOLIDAYS?

The Boohamas

WHAT SOUND DO WITCHES MAKE WHEN THEY EAT CEREAL?

Snap, Cackle & Pop!

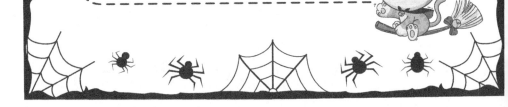

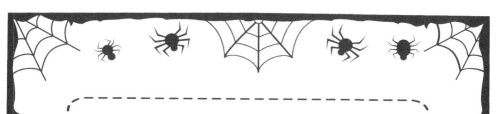

WHAT DID ONE GHOST SAY TO THE OTHER?

Get a life!

WHERE DO FASHIONABLE GHOSTS SHOP?

Bootiques.

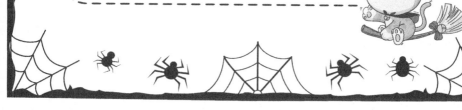

HOW DO YOU KNOW VAMPIRES LOVE BASEBALL?

They turn into bats every night.

WHERE DO GHOSTS LIKE TO TRAVEL ON VACATION?

The Dead Sea!

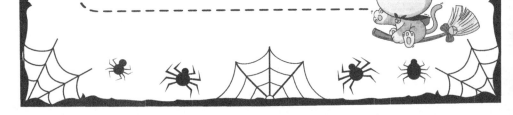

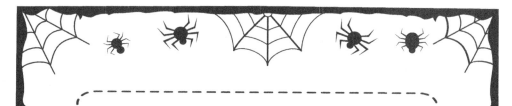

THE SKELETON DIDN'T MIND THAT EVERYONE CALLED HIM A BONEHEAD.

WHY DID THE SKELETON CLIMB UP THE TREE?

Because a dog was after his bones!

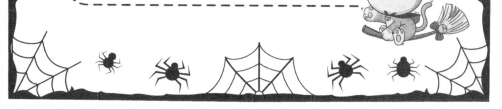

WHAT DO SKELETONS FLY AROUND IN?

A scareplane or
a skelecopter.

WHAT DID THE FISHERMAN SAY ON HALLOWEEN?

Trick or trout.

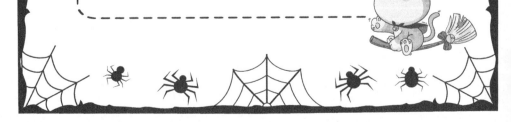

WHAT DO YOU CALL A FAT PUMPKIN?

A plumpkin.

Knock, knock!
WHO'S THERE?
Boo.
BOO WHO?
Don't cry! I didn't mean to scare you.

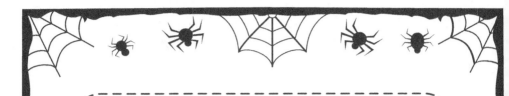

WHY ARE GHOSTS SO BAD
AT TELLING LIES?

Because you can see
right through them.

WHERE DO BABY GHOSTS
GO DURING THE DAY?

Day-scare.

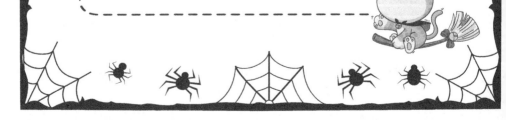

WHAT DID THE BIRD SAY ON HALLOWEEN?

Twick or tweet.

WHAT DID THE MOTHER GHOST SAY TO THE BABY GHOST AS THEY DROVE DOWN THE STREET?

Buckle your sheet belt!

WHAT DO YOU CALL TWO WITCHES SHARING AN APARTMENT?

Broommates.

WHAT'S A GHOST'S FAVORITE DESSERT?

I scream.

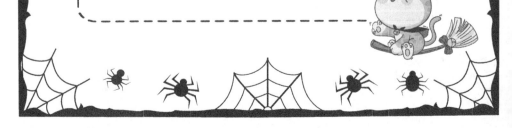

WHAT'S A SKELETON'S FAVORITE INSTRUMENT?

A sax-a-bone.

WHY ARE GRAVEYARDS SO NOISY?

Because of all the coffin.

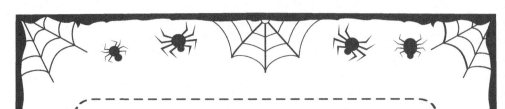

HOW DO GHOSTS SEARCH THE WEB?

They use ghoul-gle.

WHY DO DEMONS AND GHOULS HANG OUT TOGETHER?

Because demons are a ghoul's best friend!

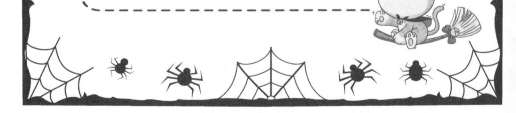

WANNA KNOW WHY SKELETONS ARE SO CALM?

Because nothing gets under their skin.

HOW DO YOU FIX A DAMAGED JACK-O-LANTERN?

You use a pumpkin patch!

WHY DIDN'T THE ZOMBIE GO TO SCHOOL?

He felt rotten!

WHAT HAS HUNDREDS OF EARS BUT CAN'T HEAR A THING?

A cornfield!

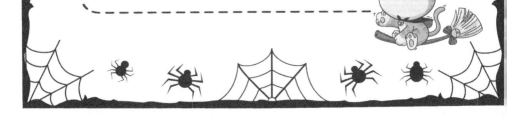

THE SKELETON CANCELED THE GALLERY SHOWING OF HIS SKULL-PTURES BECAUSE HIS HEART WASN'T IN IT.

WHAT TYPE OF PLATES DO SKELETONS LIKE TO USE?

Bone china.

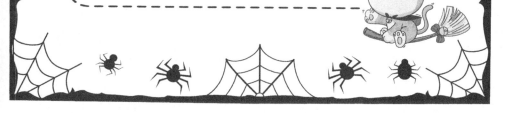

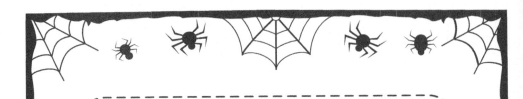

WHAT GOES AROUND A HAUNTED
HOUSE AND NEVER STOPS?

A fence.

WHAT DID ONE THIRSTY VAMPIRE
SAY TO THE OTHER AS THEY
WERE PASSING THE MORGUE?

Let's stop in for
a cool one!

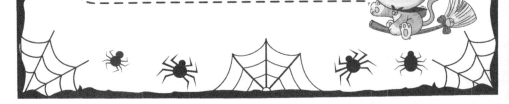

WHAT IS A VAMPIRE'S PET PEEVE?

A Tourniquet!

WHERE DO GHOSTS LIKE TO TRICK-OR-TREAT?

Dead ends.

THE SKELETON DECIDED TO BONE UP ON THE FACTS FOR THE BIG EXAM.

WHO DO MONSTERS BUY COOKIES FROM?

Ghoul scouts.

HOW DOES A VAMPIRE ENTER HIS HOUSE?

Through the bat flap!

WHY IS A CEMETERY A GREAT PLACE TO WRITE A STORY?

Because there are so many plots there!

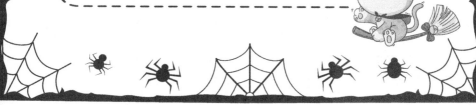

WHY DO JACK-O-LANTERNS HAVE WICKED SMILES?

Because they just had their brains scooped out!

WHY ARE THERE FENCES AROUND CEMETERIES?

Because people are dying to get in.

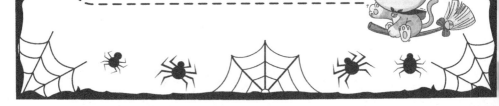

WHAT HAPPENED TO THE MAN WHO DIDN'T PAY HIS EXORCIST?

The house was repossessed.

WHAT DID THE GIRL HORSE DRESS UP AS FOR HALLOWEEN?

A night mare.

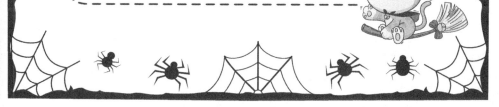

WHY DID THE WEREWOLF GO TO THE DRESSING ROOM WHEN HE SAW THE FULL MOON?

He needed to change.

WHAT DO DEMONS EAT FOR BREAKFAST?

DEVILED EGGS.

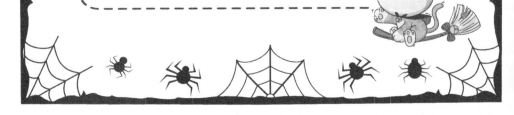

WHAT'S THE BEST WAY TO GET RID OF A DEMON?

Exorcise a lot.

WHY COULDN'T DRACULA'S WIFE GET TO SLEEP?

Because of his coffin.

WHAT IS A VAMPIRE'S FAVORITE FRUIT?

A neck-tarine.

WHY DID THE BABY WRAP IT SELF IN WHITE CLOTH STRIPS?

It was just trying to be just like its mummy.

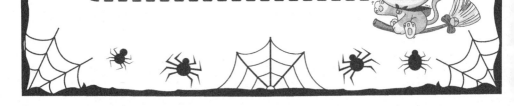

WHY DO GHOSTS LIKE TO HANG
OUT AT BARS?

Because all of the Boos.

WHAT DO YOU CALL A DANCING
GHOST?

Polka-haunt-us.

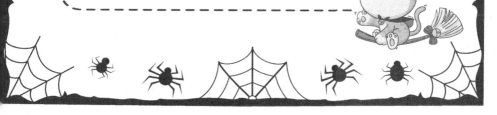

WHY DO GHOSTS HATE WHEN IT RAINS ON HALLOWEEN?

It dampens their spirits.

WHO WON THE SKELETON BEAUTY CONTEST?

No body.

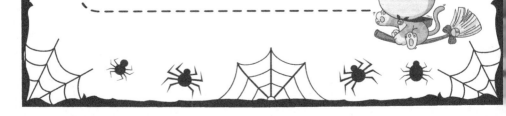

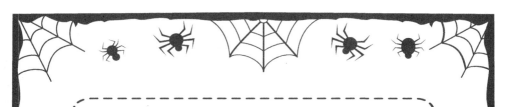

WHY DO GHOSTS MAKE THE BEST CHEERLEADERS?

Because they have spirit.

WHAT DO YOU GET WHEN YOU CROSS BAMBI WITH A GHOST?

Bamboo.

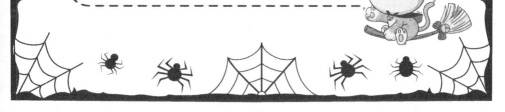

WHAT KIND OF MONSTER IS THE BEST DANCER?

The boogieman.

WHAT IS A WITCH'S FAVORITE CLASS?

Spelling!

WHAT DO YOU CALL A CHICKEN THAT HAUNTS YOUR HOUSE?

A poultrygeist.

WHY DO GHOSTS LOVE GOING TO SIX FLAGGS?

Because they can ride lots of roller-GHOST-ers.

HOW DO MONSTERS LIKE
THEIR EGGS?

Terror-fried.

WHY DIDN'T THE COFFEE BEAN
GO TO THE HALLOWEEN PARTY?

Because it was grounded.

WHO ARE THE WEREWOLF'S COUSINS?

The what-wolf and then when-wolf.

WHY DIDN'T THE MUMMY HAVE ANY FRIENDS?

He was too wrapped up in himself.

WHY DIDN'T THE VAMPIRE ATTACK TAYLOR SWIFT?

Because she had bad blood.

WHAT IS A GHOST'S FAVORITE MEAL?

Spook-ghetti.

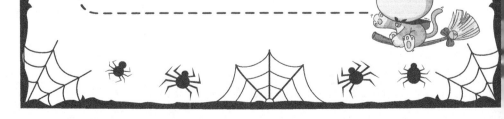

WHAT DO WITCHES USE ON THEIR HAIR?

Scare-spray.

WHY DO GIRL GHOSTS GO ON DIETS?

So they can keep their ghoulish figures.

Grab Your 60 FREE Halloween Jokes!

Keep the Halloween magic alive with exclusive jokes that are sure to make you and your family roar with laughter! Just scan the QR code below to download your free pages instantly.

It's quick and easy—get yours now!

Loved our Halloween Joke Book?

Your feedback means a lot!

Share your thoughts and help other parents find it! Scan the QR code below to Leave us a quick review and let us know What is your impression of the book.

Here's how to do it in 30 seconds:

1. Open your camera app.
2. Point it at the QR code on the right.
3. Boom! The review page opens instantly!

WHAT DO FEMALE GHOSTS USE TO DO THEIR MAKEUP?

Vanishing Cream!

THE FAVORED HISTORICAL RULER OF SKELETONS IS NONE OTHER THAN NAPOLEON BONE-A-PART.

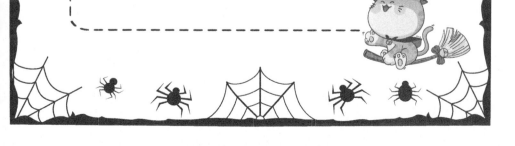

HOW DO VAMPIRES START THEIR LETTERS?

"Tomb it may concern..."

WHAT IS A RECESS AT A MORTUARY CALLED?

A Coffin Break!

THE SKELETON KNEW WHAT WOULD HAPPEN NEXT, HE COULD JUST FEEL IT IN HIS BONES.

WHERE DOES DRACULA KEEP HIS MONEY?

In a blood bank.

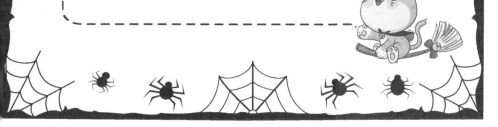

WHY ARE ALL OF SUPERMAN'S COSTUMES TIGHT?

They're all size S.

I WANTED TO TELL A SKELETON PUN, BUT I DON'T HAVE THE GUTS FOR IT.

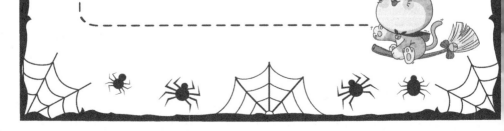

WHAT IS IT CALLED WHEN DRACULA REARRANGES HIS FURNITURE WITH HIS TEETH?

Fang-shui.

WHAT'S A GHOUL'S FAVORITE DRINK?

Anything with boos.

WHAT IS A MONSTER'S FAVORITE PET?

Creepy crawlies.

WHY DON'T MUMMIES TAKE TIME OFF?

They're afraid to unwind.

WHAT IS IN A GHOST'S NOSE?

Boo-gers.

WHAT DOES A PANDA GHOST EAT?

Bam-BOO!

WHAT DO ITALIAN GHOSTS HAVE FOR DINNER?

Spook-hetti!

WHAT DO GHOSTS USE TO DO THEIR MAKEUP?

Vanishing cream.

WHAT DO GHOSTS WEAR WHEN THEIR EYESIGHT GETS BLURRY?

Spooktacles.

WHY DO FEMALE GHOSTS GO ON A DIET?

So they can keep their ghoulish figure.

WHERE DOES A GHOST GO ON VACATION?

Mali-boo.

WHY DO DEMONS AND GHOULS HANG OUT TOGETHER?

Because demons are a ghoul's best friend!

WHY ARE GHOSTS SO BAD AT LYING?

Because you can see right through them.

WHAT DO GHOSTS USE TO WASH THEIR HAIR?

Sham-boo!

WHAT DOES A ZOMBIE CALL HIS PARENTS?

Mummy and Deady.

WHAT MONSTER PLAYS TRICKS ON HALLOWEEN?

Prank-enstein!

HOW DO GHOSTS GET THEIR HAIR TO STAY IN PLACE?

They use scare-spray.

WHAT HAPPENS WHEN A GHOST GETS LOST IN THE FOG?

He is mist.

WHY DO VAMPIRES HAVE A HARD TIME MAKING FRIENDS?

Because they are
a pain in the neck.

HOW DO YOU KNOW A SKELETON IS SICK?

He's coffin.

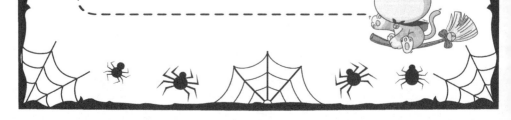

WHERE DO TODDLER GHOSTS
STAY WHEN THEIR PARENTS
ARE AT WORK?

Day scare!

WHERE DO DEVILED EGGS COME
FROM?

Evil hens.

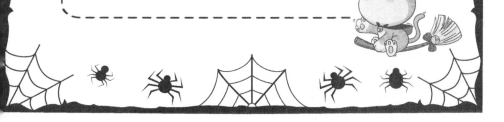

WHAT TIME IS IT WHEN THE CLOCK STRIKES 13?

Time to get a new clock.

HOW CAN YOU TELL IF A GHOST IS SCARED?

He's white as a sheet.

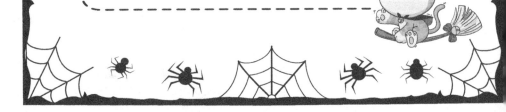

WHAT IS A ZOMBIE'S FAVORITE APPETIZER?

Finger food!

HOW DID THE JACK-O'-LANTERN BECOME A MURDERER?

He squashed someone.

WHAT DO KID GHOSTS TELL AROUND THE CAMPFIRE?

Scary human stories.

WHAT DO YOU CALL A HALLOWEEN MONSTER WHO IS REALLY BAD AT SCARING PEOPLE?

A Halloweenie!

WHAT KIND OF MUSIC DO MUMMIES LOVE?

Wrap music.

HOW DO GHOSTS WASH THEIR HAIR?

With shamboo.

WHAT'S A WITCH'S FAVORITE SUBJECT IN SCHOOL?

Spelling.

WHAT FRUIT DO SCARECROWS LOVE THE MOST?

Straw-berries.

WHAT DOES A WITCH USE
TO DO HER HAIR?

Scarespray!

WHAT ROOM DOES A GHOST
NOT NEED?

A living room.

HOW DO YOU FIX A CRACKED PUMPKIN?

A pumpkin patch.

WHEN IS IT BAD LUCK TO BE FOLLOWED BY A BLACK CAT?

If you are a mouse.

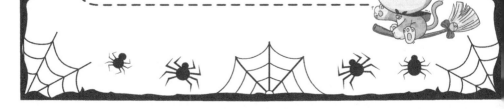

WHAT DO YOU CALL TWO WITCHES LIVING TOGETHER?

Broommates.

WHAT'S BIG, SCARY AND HAS THREE WHEELS?

A monster riding
a tricycle!

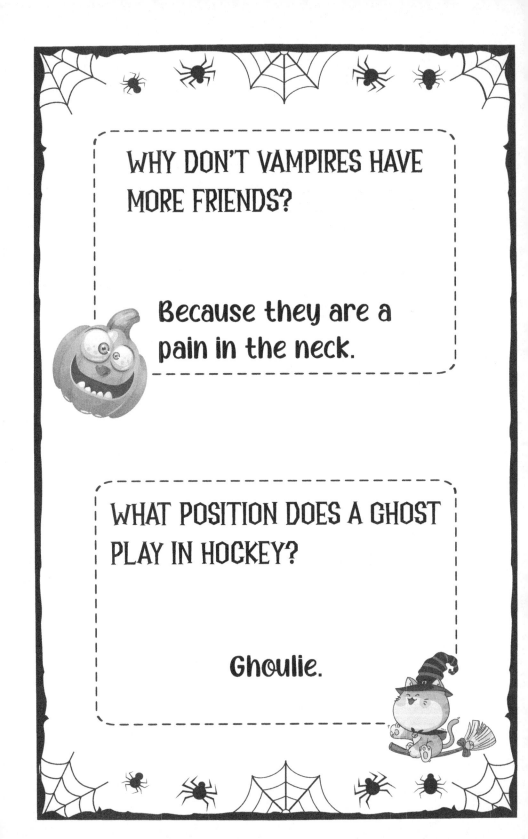

WHY DON'T VAMPIRES HAVE MORE FRIENDS?

Because they are a pain in the neck.

WHAT POSITION DOES A GHOST PLAY IN HOCKEY?

Ghoulie.

WHAT DO YOU CALL A WITCH
WHO GOES TO THE BEACH?

A sand-witch.

WHAT DO YOU GIVE A VAMPIRE
WHEN HE'S SICK?

Coffin-drops.

WHAT KINDS OF PANTS DO GHOSTS WEAR?

Boo-jeans.

WHAT IS A VAMPIRE'S FAVORITE FRUIT?

A blood orange.

WHAT DID THE LITTLE BOY SAY WHEN SHE HAD TO CHOOSE BETWEEN A TRICYCLE AND CANDY?

Trike or Treat!

WHAT INSTRUMENT DOES A SKELETON PLAY?

The trombone.

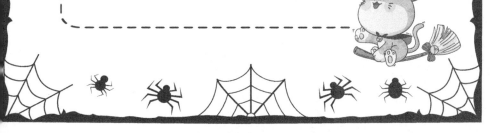

WHERE DO BABY GHOSTS GO DURING THE DAY?

Dayscare centers!

WHAT CANDY DO YOU EAT ON THE PLAYGROUND?

Recess pieces.

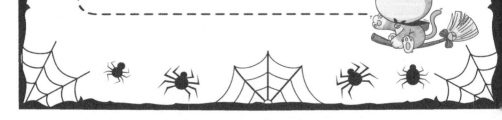

WHAT KIND OF DOG DOES DRACULA HAVE?

A blood hound.

WHAT IS A GHOST'S NOSE FULL OF?

Boooooogers!

ARE BLACK CATS BAD LUCK?

Only if you're a mouse.

WHY DO SKELETONS STAY SO CALM?

Because nothing gets under their skin.

WHY WAS THE BROOM LATE?

It over swept.

WHAT DOES AN EVIL HEN LAY?

Deviled eggs.

WHY DO GHOSTS GO ON DIETS?

So they can keep their ghoulish figures

WHY DID THE GHOST GO INTO THE BAR?

For the Boos.

WHY DID THE POLICEMAN TICKET
THE GHOST ON HALLOWEEN?

It didn't have a
haunting license.

WHY DID THE GHOST STARCH
HIS SHEET?

He wanted everyone
scared stiff.

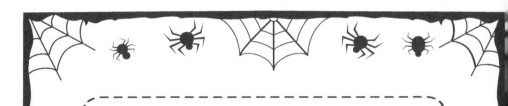

WHAT DOES A PANDA GHOST EAT?

Bam-BOO!

WHY DID THE GHOST QUIT STUDYING?

Because he was too ghoul for school.

WHERE DO GHOSTS BUY THEIR FOOD?

At the ghost-ery store!

HOW DO YOU KNOW WHEN A GHOST IS SAD?

He starts boo hooing.

HOW DO YOU KNOW YOU'VE BEEN GHOSTED?

The poltergeist doesn't text you back.

WHAT KIND OF HORSE DO GHOSTS RIDE?

A night-mare

HOW DO GHOSTS SEND LETTERS?

Through the ghost office.

WHY DID THE HEADLESS HORSEMAN GO INTO BUSINESS?

He wanted to get ahead in life.

WHY COULDN'T THE MUMMY GO TO SCHOOL WITH THE WITCH?

He couldn't spell.

HOW DO MUMMIES TELL THEIR FUTURE?

They read their horror-scope.

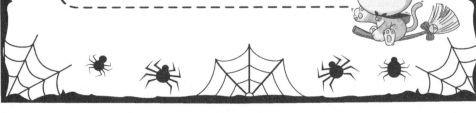

WHERE DOES A MUMMY GO ON ACATION?

The Dead Sea.

WHAT DO YOU CALL A MUMMY COVERED IN CHOCOLATE AND NUTS?

A Pharaoh Roche.

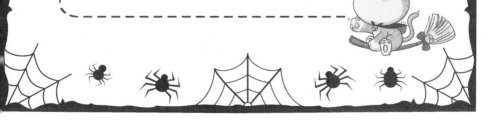

WHY DO SKELETONS HAVE LOW
SELF-ESTEEM?

They have no body
to love.

WHAT DO YOU CALL A WITCH'S
GARAGE?

A broom closet.

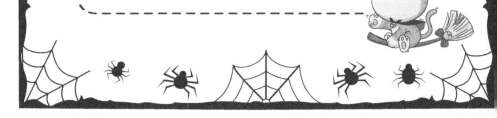

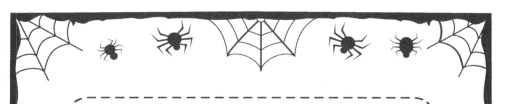

WHY DID THE PUMPKIN TAKE A DETOUR?

To avoid a seedy part of town.

WHY DON'T ZOMBIES LIKE PIRATES?

They're too salty.

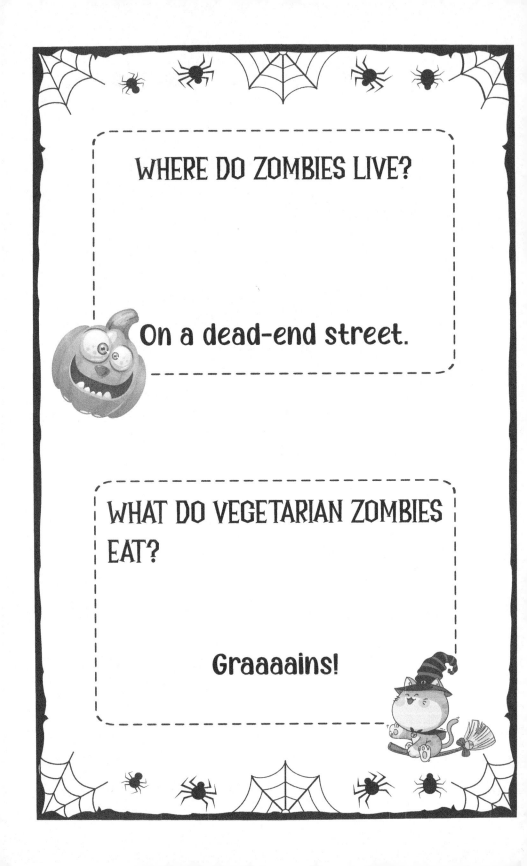

WHERE DO ZOMBIES LIVE?

On a dead-end street.

WHAT DO VEGETARIAN ZOMBIES EAT?

Graaaains!

HOW DO VAMPIRES START THEIR LETTERS?

Tomb it may concern.

WHAT TYPE OF PLANTS DO WELL ON ALL HALLOW'S EVE?

Bam-BOO!

WHAT'S A PUMPKIN'S FAVORITE GENRE?

Pulp fiction.

WHY DO GHOSTS MAKE THE BEST CHEERLEADERS?

They have a lot of spirit!

WHAT'S IT CALLED WHEN
A VAMPIRE HAS TROUBLE
WITH HIS HOUSE?

A grave problem.

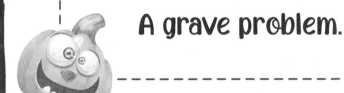

WHY CAN'T THE BOY GHOST
HAVE BABIES?

Because he has
a Hallo-weenie.

Thank You for Reading!

I want to personally thank you for choosing this book and supporting my work. Your purchase means the world to me, and I truly hope this book brought joy and creativity to your Halloween season!

Unlock Exclusive Discounts & Special Offers!

To show my appreciation, I'd like to offer you something special:

As a thank you for being an awesome reader, I'm offering exclusive discounts on my best-selling books! Just sign up for my email list to unlock:

- 20% off your next book purchase
- Early access to new releases
- Special offers just for subscribers

To claim your discount and discover more exciting reads, simply scan the QR code above!

You'll also receive Free Bonus content and be the first to hear about exciting new books for your family to enjoy!

Stay Creative!

Thank you for being an amazing reader and for your continued support. I look forward to bringing you more fun and engaging books!

Warmest wishes, [Anthony J. Trice]

Made in the USA
Las Vegas, NV
22 October 2024

10242719R00049